Teens
and
STDs

By Ashley Strehle Hartman

ReferencePoint
Press®

San Diego, CA

TEEN
Health
and
Safety

Content Consultant: Elissa M. Barr, Professor, Department of Public Health, University of North Florida

LIBRARY OF CONGRESS CATALOGING-IN-PUBLICATION DATA

Name: Strehle Hartman, Ashley, 1986– author.
Title: Teens and STDs / by Ashley Strehle Hartman.
Description: San Diego, CA : ReferencePoint Press, Inc., [2019] | Series:
    Teen Health and Safety | Audience: Grade 9 to 12. | Includes
    bibliographical references and index.
Identifiers: LCCN 2018011553 (print) | LCCN 2018012119 (ebook) | ISBN
    9781682825143 (eBook) | ISBN 9781682825136 (hardback)
Subjects: LCSH: Teenagers—Health and hygiene—Juvenile literature. |
    Sexually transmitted diseases—Prevention—Juvenile literature. | Sexually
    transmitted diseases—Treatment—Juvenile literature. | Sexual
    health—Juvenile literature.
Classification: LCC RJ140 (ebook) | LCC RJ140 .S77 2019 (print) | DDC
    614.5/470835—dc23
LC record available at https://lccn.loc.gov/2018011553

CONTENTS

OLIVIA'S STORY

Olivia is 16 years old. She is a junior in high school. She's taking some of her hardest classes ever this semester—honors English, calculus, and chemistry to name just a few. Last week she became captain of her junior varsity soccer team. Later this month, Olivia's mom is taking her on her first college visit. Between school, soccer, preparing for college, and her part-time job, Olivia is very busy.

But when she does have free time, Olivia likes to spend it with her boyfriend, Mason. He's Olivia's first serious boyfriend. Olivia knows Mason had a few other serious relationships before they got together. A few weeks ago, Olivia and Mason had sex for the first time. They didn't use protection. Olivia had meant to, but in the moment, she and Mason were not prepared. Now Olivia is worried. She feels a bit strange. She has noticed a burning sensation when she goes to the bathroom. This hasn't happened to her before.

Usually Olivia would ask her mom about her problem. Then the two of them would make Olivia an appointment with her family doctor. This time though, Olivia is worried she might have a sexually transmitted disease (STD). She doesn't want to talk to her mom about it and she doesn't want to visit the family doctor she has seen since she was a kid. Olivia doesn't know what to do.

Talking with a trusted adult is helpful for many teens struggling with an STD. Teens and adults can work together to figure out how to handle an STD.

Teens Affected by STDs

Olivia is not alone. The Centers for Disease Control and Prevention (CDC) estimates that young people between the ages of fifteen and twenty-four make up about 25 percent of the people who are sexually active. But in the United States, they account for one-half of the 20 million new STD infections that occur each year. STDs affect sexually active people of all ages, but according to the CDC, they "take a particularly heavy toll on young people."[1] This happens for many reasons. In some cases, teens are at greater risk of catching STDs because they are more likely to have unprotected sex and be in more relationships. Teens are also vulnerable because, like Olivia, they may be reluctant to talk to their parents or family health-care providers if they think they may have an STD. If these barriers prevent teens from seeking treatment, the consequences of the STD can worsen over time.

The burning sensation Olivia gets when she urinates could be caused by chlamydia, one of the most common STDs in the United States. It can be spread by oral, vaginal, or anal sexual activity with an infected person, and it is especially common among young people. One in twenty sexually active women between the ages of fourteen and twenty-four has chlamydia. As is the case with many STDs, chlamydia often shows no symptoms. "A lot of STDs are asymptomatic [showing no signs or symptoms] or the symptoms are so mild, you wouldn't necessarily know they're STDs," explained Dr. Idries Abdur-Rahman, who is an ob-gyn.[2] It may seem like a good thing when an STD does not show symptoms, but that may lead the infection to go undetected until it causes more serious health problems.

"A lot of STDs are asymptomatic [showing no signs or symptoms] or the symptoms are so mild, you wouldn't necessarily know they're STDs."[2]

—Dr. Idries Abdur-Rahman, ob-gyn

Protecting Teens from STDs

Teenagers can protect themselves from STDs and

their related health problems by practicing abstinence. According to Planned Parenthood, a nonprofit focused on reproductive issues, many people define abstinence as "not doing ANY kind of sexual stuff with another person, including vaginal, oral, and anal sex."[3] However, if teens do decide to participate in sexual activity, there are steps they can take to make these experiences safer.

"There's a lot you can do to protect yourself and your partner (or partners)," said Dr. Vanessa Cullins, Planned Parenthood Federation of America's vice president of external medical affairs. For example, if teens use condoms correctly each time they have a sexual experience, it can provide "excellent protection against STDs," Cullins explained. "Getting tested for STDs regularly is another excellent way to protect your health and take control of your sex life," she said.[4]

Teens can also better protect themselves from STDs by learning how these diseases are spread and how to avoid catching them. According to Dr. Eloisa Llata, a medical epidemiologist with the CDC's division of STD prevention, talking about STDs is one way to help prevent their spread among teens. "Everyone should talk more—and more openly— about STDs in order to raise awareness and reduce stigma," suggested Llata.[5] When teens are encouraged to talk about STDs more openly, they may be more likely to get help for an STD when they need it—either for its prevention or treatment.

> **"Everyone should talk more—and more openly— about STDs in order to raise awareness and reduce stigma."[5]**
>
> —Dr. Eloisa Llata, medical epidemiologist

Chapter 1

WHAT ARE STDS?

STDs are infections spread through the intimate exchange of bodily fluids or skin to skin contact. They are sometimes called sexually transmitted infections (STIs). STDs are very common and often affect teens and young adults. One-half of sexually active people get an STD by the time they are twenty-five.

Chlamydia is one of most common STDs, along with gonorrhea, herpes, pubic lice, trichomoniasis, and the human papilloma virus (HPV). Other, less common, but serious STDs include hepatitis B, syphilis, and the human immunodeficiency virus (HIV) which leads to acquired immunodeficiency syndrome (AIDS). There are more than twenty-four different infections that are spread primarily through sexual activity. These infections come in three types: bacterial, viral, and parasitic.

Bacterial infections are caused by single-celled organisms called bacteria. Bacteria can live in many environments and can be helpful and harmful. While good bacteria live in people's intestines and help them digest food, harmful bacteria can cause health problems such as strep throat. Chlamydia, gonorrhea, and syphilis are caused by bacteria.

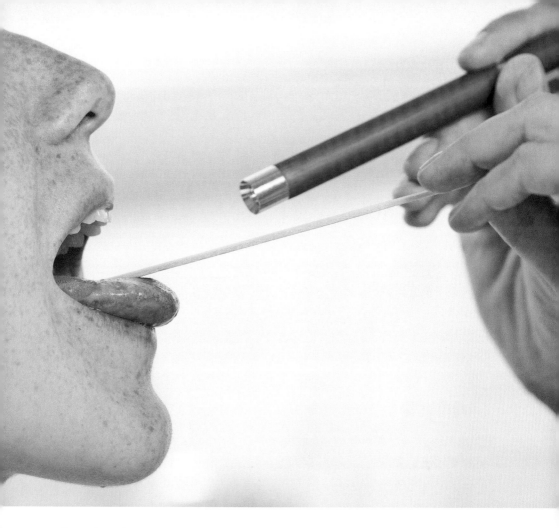

Strep throat is caused by the bacteria group Streptococcus. *Bacteria can be harmful to people's health.*

Viral infections are caused by viruses. At one-millionth of an inch long, viruses are 1,000 times smaller than bacteria. Viruses don't have the ability to make the chemical reactions needed for life. Instead, they need living hosts to survive. Viruses get into people's bodies, take over some of their cells, and make these cells produce more of the virus. This triggers people's immune systems to raise their body temperature and create inflammation. Both of these processes help destroy viruses but make people feel sick. The common cold and chicken pox are caused by viruses. Genital herpes, HPV, HIV/AIDS and hepatitis B are also caused by viruses.

Parasitic infections are caused by parasites. These are organisms that live in, or on, host organisms. They use the host organism to survive, either feeding on it directly or taking its food. Two of the most common STDs caused by parasites are pubic lice and trichomoniasis.

The symptoms and treatment for STDs depend on whether the infection is caused by a bacterium, virus, or parasite. There are no cures for viral STDs. Instead, their treatment focuses on minimizing symptoms or slowing the progress of the infection. STDs that are caused by bacteria or parasites can be cured with medication. Many people with these STDs do not show obvious symptoms, so they may have these infections for years without realizing it. Once the disease is diagnosed, medication may stop the infection. However, it cannot fix the damage that happened before the treatment started.

Chlamydia

Chlamydia is caused by the bacterium *Chlamydia trachomatis*. It is the most commonly reported bacterial STD. More than 1.5 million cases of chlamydia were reported to the CDC in 2016 and an estimated 2.86 million infections occur each year. People between the ages of fifteen and twenty-four make up almost two-thirds of new chlamydia infections. Chlamydia is so common among teenagers, in part, because of the way girls' bodies are developed at this age. Leah Millheiser, who is the director of the Female Sexual Medicine Program at Stanford University and an ob-gyn, noted that girls of this age are more at risk for chlamydia because of the cells on their cervix during that time. For that reason, sexually active women younger than twenty-five are encouraged to get tested for chlamydia regularly.

Another reason people should get a chlamydia test each year is because the disease is hard to detect otherwise. Many people with chlamydia do not know they have it unless they are tested for it or a sexual partner tells them they have been exposed. Chlamydia is often called a silent disease because many individuals do not show symptoms. "The interesting thing about symptoms of chlamydia is that, in women, most people don't experience them," explained June Gupta, a women's health nurse practitioner and the associate director of medical standards for Planned Parenthood Federation of America.[6]

If chlamydia symptoms appear in women, they usually include vaginal discharge that may be yellow, pain during intercourse, pain in the pelvis or lower belly, and a burning sensation during urination. Gupta noted that pelvic or lower belly pain could be a sign that the infection has progressed—moving from the cervix into the uterus.

> "The interesting thing about symptoms of chlamydia is that, in women, most people don't experience them."[6]
>
> —June Gupta, a women's health nurse practitioner and the associate director of medical standards for Planned Parenthood Federation of America

Untreated chlamydia may also cause more long-term problems for girls and women. In an October 2016 report, the CDC noted, "Both young men and young women are heavily affected by STDs/STIs—but young women face the most serious long-term health consequences. It is estimated that undiagnosed STDs/STIs cause infertility in more than 20,000 women each year."[7] Men with chlamydia may experience mild irritation on the penis and a gray to white discharge from their genitals. Chlamydia can also cause rectal inflammation, pink eye, upper respiratory infections, and infections in the urinary tract and cervix.

Gonorrhea

Gonorrhea, occasionally called the clap, is caused by the bacterium *Neisseria gonorrhoeae*, which infects mucous membranes in the

Infertility is a problem that many couples face. It can weigh heavily on a couple's mind when they want to have children.

reproductive tract. In women, this affects the cervix, uterus, and fallopian tubes; and in both men and women, it can affect the urethra. Gonorrhea can also attack the mucous membranes in the rectum, mouth, eyes, and throat.

Like chlamydia, gonorrhea is a very common STD. In the fall of 2016, the CDC reported there was an all-time high for rates of gonorrhea, chlamydia, and syphilis. There are more than 800,000 new gonorrhea infections each year in the United States. More than 570,000 of these infections affect people between the ages of fifteen and twenty-four.

Like chlamydia, gonorrhea can exist in people's bodies without symptoms for some time. However, symptoms may appear a few days to several weeks after people have been exposed to the bacteria. In women, the symptoms of gonorrhea can include increased vaginal discharge, bleeding between periods, and pain when urinating. These symptoms can often be mistaken for a bladder or vaginal infection. Men with gonorrhea may experience a burning sensation when they urinate. They may also notice a white, yellow, or green discharge from their penis. In some cases, men with gonorrhea may also get painful or swollen testicles. Gonorrhea, like other bacterial STDs, can be treated and cured with medication. However, if left untreated, gonorrhea can cause long-term health problems such as infertility.

Syphilis

Syphilis is caused by the bacterium *Treponema pallidum* which attacks people's nervous systems and organs. This bacterium was identified in 1905, but syphilis has a much longer history. It is a very old disease. One theory on the origins of syphilis proposes that Christopher Columbus and his sailors brought syphilis to Europe after their voyage to the Americas. In the 1490s, an epidemic of syphilis hit Europe, where it was called the pox.

In the 1940s, scientists developed the antibiotic penicillin, which was effective in treating syphilis. This led to a dramatic reduction in syphilis cases. Doctors in the United States thought they had almost entirely eliminated the STD. They believed they had made syphilis a "disease of the past," explained Dr. Gail Bolan, director of CDC's Division of STD Prevention. "I remember a professor in medical school explaining what it was to us but then said 'You'll never see it.'"[8]

However, between 2015 and 2016 the rates of syphilis increased almost 18 percent. The majority of these cases occurred in men who have sex with men. There was also an increase in the number of women who were passing syphilis to their newborns. In 2013, the rates of syphilis reported for boys between the ages of fifteen and nineteen was the highest it had been since 1995. Bolan suggested that a lack of funding for STD prevention and education may be part of the reason for the increase. Syphilis earned the nickname the great pretender because its symptoms often look like those of other diseases. This can lead to problems with diagnosis because patients don't know the symptoms of syphilis and when to get help. "The fact that so many of these diseases are asymptomatic . . . mean that men and women aren't getting into their doctor to be tested," Bolan explained. "We need to get the word out that everyone needs a yearly checkup. And we need to re-educate physicians to look for signs of such 'ancient' diseases as syphilis."[9]

> **"We need to get the word out that everyone needs a yearly checkup. And we need to re-educate physicians to look for signs of such 'ancient' diseases as syphilis."[9]**
>
> —Dr. Gail Bolan, director of CDC's Division of STD Prevention

Syphilis has different distinct stages. In the first, or primary, stage of syphilis, a small, firm, painless ulcer called a chancre appears. It usually shows up at the site where the infection entered the body. In the secondary stage of syphilis, sufferers usually develop a non-itchy rash. It usually shows up on their hands or feet, but it can occasionally cover more of their body. Latent syphilis is a stage of untreated syphilis in which there are no obvious symptoms. The late stage of syphilis, called the tertiary stage, is uncommon, but can show up anywhere in a person's body. It can cause serious problems such as blindness, deafness, mental illness, heart disease, neurological problems, and even death.

Herpes

Herpes is caused by herpes simplex virus, which has two strains—
HSV-1 and HSV-2. HSV-1, commonly referred to as cold sores, usually
affects the mouth, and HSV-2 usually affects the genitals. But each

HSV-1 IS AN INCREASING CAUSE OF GENITAL HERPES

HSV-1 is the most common form of the herpes simplex virus. According
to World Health Organization (WHO), it is estimated that two thirds of the
global population younger than age fifty has HSV-1. That's more than
3.7 billion people. In the past, HSV-1 infections were best known for
occurring in the mouth. Now, recent changes in the way people initially
contract the herpes simplex virus are making HSV-1 an important cause of
genital herpes.

In the past, people usually had their first HSV-1 infection between six
months and three years of age. These infections were usually contracted
through nonsexual contact with saliva containing the virus. For example,
young children would put a toy into their mouth that another child had
infected with their saliva. People who caught the HSV-1 oral infection
as children were then more protected against catching HSV-1 in the
genital area as adults, because they were already carrying the virus in
another form.

In developed countries, fewer people are catching HSV-1 as children
because of improved living conditions and better hygiene practices. These
people are then more vulnerable to catching HSV-1 for the first time as
adults through oral sex. Because of these changes, higher rates of HSV-1
genital infections are now being seen in North and South America, Europe,
and Western Pacific countries. Some estimates have found that HSV-1
may account for as many as one-half of all new genital herpes cases in
developed countries.

strain can occur in both locations. One person can also be infected with both strains. Herpes is very common. Each year, more than 700,000 people in the United States get a new herpes infection.

One of the reasons herpes is so common is because it is very easy to spread. "It can be passed from one partner to another and from one part of the body (like the mouth) to another (like genitals)," explained Cullins. "Brief skin-to-skin contact is all that's needed to pass the virus." Since herpes may not show symptoms for years, it is also "very difficult to know who passed it to whom," she noted.[10] Many people do not know they have herpes until the disease shows up on blood tests.

If herpes symptoms do occur, the main symptom is usually small, red bumps or blisters which can appear on the penis, vagina, vulva, cervix, buttocks, or anus. "The classic description of genital herpes is 'dew drops on a rose petal,'" explained Dr. Peter Leone, an adjunct professor of medicine at the University of North Carolina School of Medicine. "You get these little blisters on a red base that hurt—and if you have that, the probability that you have herpes is pretty high."[11] These sores usually appear between two and twenty days after a person was exposed to herpes.

> **"The classic description of genital herpes is 'dew drops on a rose petal.' You get these little blisters on a red base that hurt—and if you have that, the probability that you have herpes is pretty high."[11]**
>
> —Dr. Peter Leone, an adjunct professor of medicine at the University of North Carolina School of Medicine

Some people may find these blisters very painful, while others may just find them mildly annoying. During herpes outbreaks, people may also get flu-like symptoms such as a headache, stiff neck, sore throat, fever, and muscle aches. The first herpes outbreak usually lasts between one or two weeks. One woman detailed her experience with herpes in an anonymous *Teen Vogue* article in 2017. "I don't know exactly when I was infected—it's impossible to tell," she wrote. "But I know when I experienced my first outbreak. I awoke with a fever and everything hurt."[12] Three days later, the woman, who had gone to her physician for an STD test, found out she was positive for HSV-1. As viruses, HSV-1 and HSV-2 can't be cured with antibiotics, so the woman knew she'd have herpes for the rest of her life. Initially, she was depressed by the diagnosis, but she adjusted. "I survived, thrived and learned how to live with herpes—and if you find yourself with a herpes diagnosis, you can, and will, too. Simply stay safe and informed," she said.[13]

There is no cure for herpes. However, symptoms can be managed with antiviral medications. The disease lives on in the body even if it is not showing symptoms at the time. When the disease is reactivated, it causes outbreaks of symptoms. After the initial outbreak, herpes outbreaks usually last between three to seven days. These outbreaks can appear weeks or months after the first one and they are usually less severe than the first outbreak.

HPV

HPV refers to a group of more than one hundred viral subtypes. Of these, more than thirty are transmitted sexually. HPV is a virus that can cause genital warts, and in some cases, cancer. Like herpes, HPV is very common. It is the most common STD in the United States. Almost 80 million Americans have HPV, and most of these people are in their late teens or early twenties.

Many people with HPV also have no symptoms. When symptoms do appear, they may include painless genital warts. In women, these warts can appear on the labia, vagina, cervix, or in the anal area, as well as on the abdomen and thighs. Men may get genital warts in their urethral opening or on their penis, scrotum, anus, abdomen, or thighs. Warts may appear several weeks after sexual contact with the affected person.

The types of HPV that cause cancer do not have noticeable symptoms. They are usually only found in women when abnormal cervical cells show up on their pap tests, which involve collecting cells from the cervix and examining them under a microscope. HPV is the most common cause of cervical cancer. It can also cause vaginal, anal, penile, vulvar, and throat cancer. Each year approximately 19,000 women and 12,000 men are affected by cancers caused by HPV.

HIV/AIDS

HIV is less common than herpes and HPV, but it is more well-known because of how serious it is. HIV attacks the body's immune system. Without treatment, it progresses in the body in three stages, getting worse over time. AIDS is the final stage of HIV. It is also the most serious. The immune systems of people with AIDS are very weak so they cannot fight off illnesses the way other people can. HIV and AIDS can affect people of all ages. Young people between the ages of thirteen and twenty-four made up more than 20 percent of all new HIV diagnoses in the United States in 2016.

As with other types of STDs, HIV can often show no symptoms. Many people with HIV have no symptoms for up to ten years after their infection. Other people develop flu-like symptoms a few months after their infection, including headaches, fatigue, enlarged lymph nodes, and fever. As HIV progresses, it weakens the immune system. This causes other symptoms to appear. For example, at this point, many people with HIV will start having frequent yeast infections, severe herpes infections, and fevers. They may also experience weight loss, as well as short-term memory loss.

If HIV progresses to AIDS, people die from related infections or cancers they get because of their weakened immune systems. There's no cure for HIV, but there are medicines that can slow the disease's progress and treat its symptoms. These can help people with HIV or AIDS live longer, healthier lives.

Hepatitis B

Hepatitis B is a virus that causes inflammation of the liver. It is spread through the exchange of bodily fluids such as blood or semen. Unlike with other STDs, many people can get an additional layer of protection against hepatitis B. That's because, since 1990, there have been childhood vaccinations against it. However, people who are not vaccinated may develop the virus.

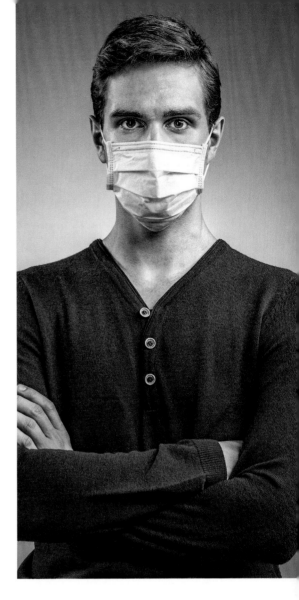

People with AIDS have weak immune systems. They need to be careful to avoid infections and germs.

Some people with hepatitis B experience only a short-term illness that shows up within six months after they are infected. Most people's immune systems will fight off hepatitis B and it will go away on its own, usually in one to two months. About one in twenty people with hepatitis B become carriers of the infection. This means their infections are chronic and they can stay contagious for life. Chronic infections of this type can lead to liver problems such as cirrhosis and liver cancer.

Pubic Lice

Pubic lice are tiny insects that are 1/16 inch (2 mm) or smaller. They are sometimes called crabs because the lice's front legs look like crab claws. These parasites are usually found on pubic hair, but they can also affect armpit hair, eyelashes, and facial hair. Pubic lice are a different kind of lice than the lice that infect the hair on people's heads.

Most cases of pubic lice are transmitted through sexual activity, but they can also be transmitted through other close contact. People can get pubic lice by sleeping in an infected bed, using an infected towel, or wearing infected clothing. Doctors can often easily diagnose pubic lice because the lice can be seen under magnification or by looking closely.

The most common symptom of pubic lice is itching, which is caused by the body's allergic reaction to the lice's bites. Black or blue spots may also appear with pubic lice and last for several days. These are also a reaction to the bites. In general, itching and discomfort are the only symptoms of pubic lice. However, in some cases, people with pubic lice may also develop other infections because they have irritated and opened their skin by scratching it.

Trichomoniasis

Trichomoniasis, sometimes called trich, is caused by the protozoan parasite *Trichomonas vaginalis*. It is the most common curable STD in young women who are sexually active. At least one out of four new trichomoniasis infections affects teenage girls.

Like pubic lice, trichomoniasis is most often spread by direct genital-to-genital contact. It can be hard for doctors to diagnose because approximately 70 percent of people with the disease do not have any symptoms. Also, trichomoniasis infections may come and go, which makes the disease harder to identify and treat.

If trich symptoms appear, women may notice a yellow-green or gray discharge from their vagina. A doctor may also notice redness or small sores on an infected woman's cervix during a pelvic exam. Most men with trichomoniasis don't have symptoms, but some men may notice irritation inside their penis, discharge, or a mild burning after they urinate or ejaculate. The symptoms of trichomoniasis usually appear five to twenty-eight days after a person was exposed to the infection.

Bacterial Vaginosis

There are some conditions that are occasionally, but not always, considered STDs. Though they can be caused or spread by other methods, these conditions are also frequently spread through sex. Three of the most common of these conditions are bacterial vaginosis (BV), molluscum contagiosum, and scabies.

BV is an infection of the vagina. It is the most common vaginal infection of women between the ages of fifteen and forty-four. According to the CDC, "Researchers do not know the cause of BV or how some women get it."[14] Though BV most often occurs in sexually active women, in rare cases, it has also developed in women who have never had sex. Though researchers are not sure

> **"Researchers do not know the cause of BV or how some women get it."[14]**
>
> —Centers for Disease Control and Prevention

of the exact cause of BV, it has been linked to an imbalance of certain kinds of bacteria in a woman's vagina. Imbalances like this happen when something upsets "the balance of power between good-guy and bad-guy bacteria," explained Dr. Mary Jane Minkin, a clinical professor of obstetrics, gynecology, and reproductive sciences at Yale Medical School.[15]

Some things that can contribute to bacterial imbalances in the vagina—and lead to increased risks of BV—are having sex with new or multiple sexual partners and douching. Douching is when women wash their vaginas with water or other fluids. The fluid is sprayed into the vagina and can create an environment for bacteria to grow. Though one in five American women between the ages of fifteen and forty-four douche, it is not recommended by doctors. It has been shown to lead to several STDs and vaginal infections.

Many women with BV do not have any symptoms. If they do occur, the main symptom is unusual vaginal discharge, which can be white or gray. It may also seem foamy or watery. Some women may also notice a fish-like odor of their discharge. Other symptoms of BV may include burning with urination and itching or irritation of the vagina. In pregnant women, BV that is left untreated and worsens can cause them to give birth to premature or low-birth weight babies.

To determine if a woman has BV, a doctor will check the patient's vagina for discharge. The doctor will also take a sample of the patient's vaginal fluid to test for the presence of BV. In women, BV is treated by antibiotics. Men who have been exposed to sexual partners with BV do not need to be treated since the condition affects the vagina. However, it is possible for BV to be transmitted between female sexual partners. If BV is not treated, it can increase women's chances of catching other STDs if they are exposed to them.

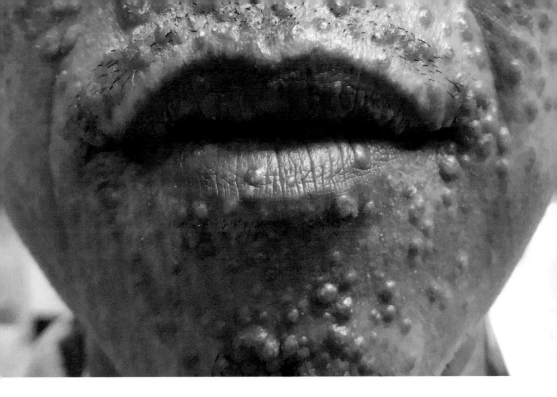

If a person with AIDS contracts molluscum contagiosum, he can develop more bumps. This is a result of his weak immune system.

Molluscum Contagiosum

Molluscum contagiosum is a viral infection of the skin. The disease is most common in children, but it can affect adults too. It can be spread through any person-to-person contact or by contact with contaminated objects. When molluscum contagiosum affects the genital area, it is considered an STD.

The virus causes people to develop round, firm, bumps that can be the size of a pin prick up to the size of a pencil eraser. These bumps are usually flesh-colored and have a small indentation on top of them. They usually appear on the face, neck, armpits, and the tops of hands in infected children. Adults who have contacted molluscum contagiosum sexually may develop bumps on their genitals, lower abdomen, and their inner and upper thighs. If these bumps are irritated, they can get red or inflamed and may become itchy.

Scabies is a curable STD. However, it can cause people a lot of discomfort.

When people scratch or injure the bumps of molluscum contagiosum, the infection can spread to other parts of their skin.

Molluscum contagiosum bumps usually get better on their own within six months to a year, even without treatment. But it is possible to develop new molluscum contagiosum bumps for up to five years. Doctors may recommend the bumps be removed, because the disease is extremely contagious when bumps are present. There are several methods of removing molluscum contagiosum, including creams and surgical methods that involve freezing off the bumps. When all the bumps are gone, people are no longer considered to be contagious with molluscum contagiosum.

Scabies

Like molluscum contagiosum, scabies is a skin condition. It is caused by parasites that infect the top layer of people's skin. Scabies can be spread with any close human contact. It can also be spread through infected clothes, towels, or sheets. For that reason, scabies is common in crowded places such as prisons, nursing homes, and day cares. People usually can't get scabies from limited contact with an infected person. For example, people are unlikely to get scabies from a handshake or hug. Scabies needs lots of close contact in order to spread. That is why it is most often spread through sexual activity.

The main symptom of scabies is itching, which can be intense and is often worse at night. People may also develop rashes that have blisters, scales, or bumps like pimples. Some people may also see raised lines on their skin, which are caused by scabies mites moving under the skin's surface. People usually get scabies rashes between their fingers or in the bends of their wrists, elbows, or knees. Scabies rashes may also appear in the groin and on the penis and scrotum. Belly buttons, breasts, thighs, buttocks, shoulder blades, and waists may also be affected. Though scabies can be very uncomfortable, it is not usually considered dangerous.

Scabies can be cured with creams or pills prescribed by a doctor. People who have been infected by scabies should also treat their bedding, towels, or clothing that may have been infected by the parasite. These items should be washed on the hottest possible setting and dried on the hot cycle for at least twenty minutes. People who have scabies should notify anyone they have had close contact with while infected, including all of their sexual partners.

Teens Can Help Prevent STDs

There are many different kinds of STDs. Some of them cause short-term discomfort. Others can have serious, long-term consequences. They are caused by different organisms and spread in different ways. One thing all STDs have in common is their ability to affect almost anyone. A thorough understanding of STDs is a teen's best tool to avoid contraction.

Chapter 2

WHAT CAUSES STDS?

STDs are spread by vaginal, oral, and anal sex, as well as any type of genital-to-genital contact. How quickly and effectively these diseases spread depends on the type of sexual activity involved, whether protection is used, and whether infected people receive appropriate health care.

To monitor the spread of STDs in teens, the CDC looks at teens' sexual activity with its Youth Risk Behavior Surveys (YRBS) given to teens in grades 9 to 12. In the surveys, teens are asked about six categories of health behavior, including those related to STDs. These anonymous surveys have been conducted by the CDC every two years since 1991. In the study released in 2015, the CDC found that, nationwide, a large number of high school students had had sexual intercourse.

According to a study published in the *Journal of Adolescent Health* in 2017, today's teens and young adults are engaging in more oral and anal sex than their peers from twenty years ago. The study is based on a series of surveys of heterosexual, sexually active British residents between the ages of sixteen to twenty-four. These surveys have been conducted once each decade for the past three decades. Vaginal sex was found to be the most common sexual act throughout

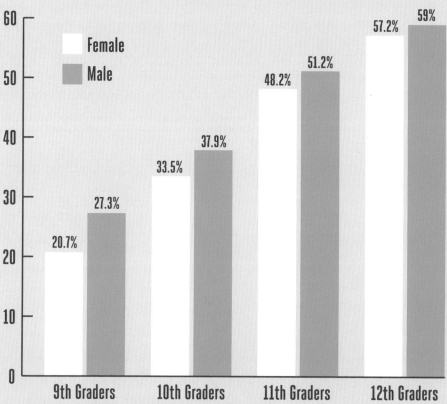

TEENS AND SEXUAL INTERCOURSE

Female

Male

Grade	Female	Male
9th Graders	20.7%	27.3%
10th Graders	33.5%	37.9%
11th Graders	48.2%	51.2%
12th Graders	57.2%	59%

This graph shows the number of high school students who reported having sexual intercourse, broken down by gender and grade level. As the graph shows, the number of students who have had sexual intercourse usually increases with age. For example, more 12th grade students have had sexual intercourse than 9th grade students. The graph also shows that there is little difference between the percentage of male and female students who have had sexual intercourse.

all the surveys, but the number of people who reported having also had oral and anal sex has grown over time. The number of people surveyed who said they'd had vaginal, oral, and anal sex within the last year more than doubled between the surveys completed in 1990 and 2012.

More of today's teens are engaged in sexual activities other than vaginal intercourse. Some teens incorrectly think that having only nonvaginal intercourse will protect them from STDs. This is not true. STDs can be spread by virtually any kind of sexual contact. "Anywhere there's a moist environment, an STD can be transmitted," explained Dr. Sherry Ross, ob-gyn and women's health expert.[16]

Though STDs can be spread through these sex acts, many teens don't take the steps necessary to prevent STDs. For example, teens may not use condoms during oral sex to prevent the spread of STDs. "Many studies show that adolescents and young adults are unaware of the health risks associated with oral sex," said Giuseppina Valle Holway, a sociology professor at The University of Tampa in Florida who coauthored a report on the subject for the *Journal of Adolescent Health*.[17] Holway and her coauthor Stephanie Hernandez looked at reports of heterosexual oral sex and the use of condoms among Americans between the ages of fifteen and twenty-four. They found that, among the more than 7,000 people studied, more than one-half of them had engaged in oral sex in the last year. However, only 8 percent of the women and 9 percent of the men used a condom during the act.

> **"Anywhere there's a moist environment, an STD can be transmitted."[16]**
>
> —Sherry Ross, MD, ob-gyn and women's health expert

Proper Protection for All Sexual Activity

In general, teens aren't using condoms enough—no matter what type of sex they're having. In their YRBS surveys, the CDC found that 43 percent of sexually active high school students hadn't used a condom the last time they had sex. In a similar report on condom usage in 2017, the CDC asked participants between the ages of fifteen and nineteen whether they used a condom every time they had sexual intercourse during the past year. About 36 percent of females and 54 percent of males said they had. The survey also found that in the same age group, about 15.7 percent of women and 7 percent of men said they had never used a condom in the past year.

CONDOMS

People can purchase condoms at most stores, online, or in vending machines. Everyone can buy condoms because they don't require prescriptions and don't have age restrictions. Teens can also get condoms at their doctors' offices and from community health and Planned Parenthood centers. Condoms can be free when they are given by a doctor or health center and, when purchased, they are relatively inexpensive.

Condom costs depends on the brand, but most of them cost about one dollar each. The majority of condoms are made from latex, but there are condoms made of soft plastics for people allergic to latex. Most condoms offer similar protection against pregnancy and STDs, despite the brand or type. Just check the box or wrapper to make sure the condoms offer protection against STDs and pregnancy. Condoms made from animal membrane like lambskin only prevent against pregnancy, not STDs.

Though condoms are designed to last a long time, it is important to store them properly. They should be kept in a cool, dry place away from direct sunlight. Since excessive heat can damage a condom, don't keep them in places that are warm such as pockets, wallets, cars, or bathrooms. Before using a condom, make sure it doesn't have holes in the packaging or condom itself. Also, make sure it's not past the condom's expiration date.

Dr. Dustin Costescu, a family planning specialist, said that many teens don't use condoms because they think they're not at risk for catching STDs. "We know teens underestimate the rates," he explained. "A lot of people don't see themselves [at risk] because they date one person, and they think they are at a lower risk compared to those who have multiple sexual partners."[18]

Costescu suggested that the way people talk about condoms may be another reason for teens' low condom usage. He said many teens are taught to see condoms as only protection against pregnancy, when their usage is just as important to protect against STDs. This theory is supported by a 2017 University of Minnesota report on teen sexual health. The report was written by Jill Farris, the university's director of adolescent sexual health. The report found that the rates of pregnancy among fifteen to nineteen-year-olds has dropped by 70 percent since 1990, while the STD rates among teens have gone up 40 percent for gonorrhea and 15 percent for chlamydia. "Fewer young people are using condoms," Farris said. "Sometimes young people will start using them, but once one of the partners gets on a long-term method of birth control, condom use will stop."[19] When teens do this, they are protected against pregnancy, but not STDs. This could account for the decrease in teen pregnancy, as well as the increase in teen STDs.

Condoms are the only birth control method that also protects people from STDs. Male condoms are made of latex or polyurethane (a kind of plastic). They are thin and stretchy and can expand into a pouch.

> **"Fewer young people are using condoms. Sometimes young people will start using them, but once one of the partners gets on a long-term method of birth control, condom use will stop."[19]**
>
> —Jill Farris, director of adolescent sexual health at the University of Minnesota

They are used to cover a penis during sexual intercourse. Before vaginal or anal sex, a male condom should be put on the tip of the erect penis. Many condoms come with a reservoir tip at the top, but if the condom doesn't have one of these, users should pinch the tip of the condom enough to leave about a half-inch space. Semen will collect here. While holding the tip of the condom, users should unroll the condom all the way to the base of the erect penis.

After ejaculation and before the penis is not erect, users should grip the rim of the condom while withdrawing from sexual contact, then pull the condom off of the penis. They should make sure that semen does not come out of the condom. To ensure that other people will not handle the condom, the condom should be wrapped in a tissue and put in the trash. If sexual partners feel the condom break at any point during sexual contact, they should stop immediately, withdraw, remove and dispose of the broken condom, and appropriately put on a new condom before continuing sexual activity. If sexual partners are using lubrication during sexual activity, they should be sure to use water-based products. Oil-based products can weaken the latex in condoms, so they should not be used. Oil-based lubricants include things such as mineral oil, massage oils, cooking oils, body lotions, shortening, or petroleum jelly.

During vaginal intercourse, male condoms create a barrier between the penis and the vagina. Sperm that is ejaculated from the penis during intercourse is collected inside the condom. This prevents the sperm from getting into the vagina, where it could possibly travel through the female reproductive tract to meet an egg and cause pregnancy. Male condoms also prevent against many STDs by covering the penis during sexual intercourse. This prevents the condom wearer from spreading STDs that may be present in his semen. It also protects the wearer from the STDs his partner may have in her vaginal fluids, as well as STDs that may be spread during anal sex. By covering the penis, male condoms also reduce the amount of skin-to-skin contact people have during sexual intercourse. This limits the spread of STDs, because some of them, such as herpes and genital warts, can be spread by skin-to-skin intimate contact.

But condoms shouldn't just be used during vaginal intercourse. They should also be used during oral and anal sex. The effectiveness of condoms in preventing STDs has been shown in laboratory studies. But in order for condoms to provide this protection, they have to be used each time people participate in sexual activity. The CDC has said that inconsistent use of condoms "can lead to STD acquisition because transmission can occur with a single sex act with an infected partner."[20]

Oral Sex and STDs

The risk of catching or spreading STDs through oral sex depends on the type of STD, the type of oral sex, and the number of times oral sex is performed. However, several STDs are known to be spread through oral sex, including chlamydia, gonorrhea, syphilis, herpes, HPV, trichomoniasis, and HIV. Despite this, many young adults who engage in oral sex "do not perceive they are at risk of contracting a sexually transmitted infection," according to Erin Moore, a professor of human sexuality.[21]

STDs that spread through oral sex can develop in the mouth or throat. For example, a person who gives oral sex to a partner who has an STD on their genital or rectal area may develop that STD in his or her mouth. People who have a STD infection in their mouth may then spread that STD to other peoples' genitals or rectal areas by giving them oral sex. In some cases, such as with gonorrhea, infections of the throat can be harder to treat than urinary, rectal, or genital infections. STDs that develop in the mouth can also spread to

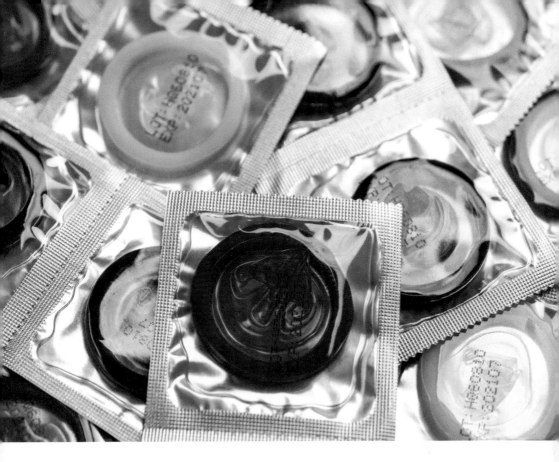

Condoms are one way to help prevent STDs. However, abstinence is more effective.

other parts of the body. For example, cases of syphilis that develop in the mouth can spread to the rectum or genitals. When people get mouth or throat infections of certain types of HPV, it can lead to oral or neck cancer.

The main types of protection for oral sex include condoms and dental dams. People should put a nonlubricated latex condom on the penis during oral sex on a penis. If either partner is allergic to latex, they should use a plastic or polyurethane condom. When oral sex is being done on the vagina or anus, sexual partners should use a dental dam. A dental dam is a latex or polyurethane sheet that can be placed between the mouth and the vagina or anus during oral sex. If people do not have dental dams, they can make one with a latex or polyurethane condom. To do this, they just need to cut the tip off the condom, cut off the bottom of the condom, and cut along one side of the condom. This makes a square which can be laid flat over the vagina or anus, like a dental dam.

Anal Sex and STDs

Anal sex, like oral sex, can spread STDs. People can catch STDs, such as chlamydia and gonorrhea, from having anal sex without a condom. STDs like herpes and syphilis, which can be spread by skin to skin contact, can be spread by anal sex even if a condom is used. In addition to the risk of common STDs, anal sex without a condom can also spread additional infections. Bacterial infections such as shigella, salmonella, and E. coli, and parasites like giardia and intestinal amoebas, are spread through feces so they can be transmitted through anal sex.

According to the CDC, anal sex is also the riskiest sexual activity in terms of catching or transmitting HIV. The receptive partner in anal sex (the partner receiving the penis) is thirteen times more likely to be infected by HIV than the partner who is inserting the penis. That's because the lining of the rectum, where the penis is inserted, is thin, which allows the HIV to enter the receptive partner's body more easily. The majority of men who are infected with HIV got it through anal sex. Although the majority of women who are infected got it through vaginal sex, they can contract HIV through anal sex as well.

People can reduce their risk of HIV transmission through all sex by using condoms. The CDC has reported that people who use condoms correctly and consistently "reduced their risk of getting HIV through insertive anal sex with an HIV-positive partner, on average, by 63 percent and receptive anal sex with an HIV-positive partner, on average, by 72 percent."[22] Male condoms are also very effective in preventing other STDs if they are used throughout the entire act of anal sex.

Access to Reproductive Health Care

> **"People would rather suffer in silence than tell their parents about them having sex."**[23]
>
> —Dr. Robyn Miller, pediatrician

Not using condoms during sex leads to increased rates of STDs among teens, as does lack of access to reproductive health care. Though some teens may truly lack access to these services, other teens, like Olivia, might simply be reluctant to talk to their health-care providers. Many of these teenagers may be covered by their parents' health insurance, so they may worry that their parents will find out about their reproductive health care visit. "People would rather suffer in silence than tell their parents about them having sex," said pediatrician Dr. Robyn Miller.[23] Though teenagers believe their health is important, that belief doesn't match up with their actions, explained Dr. Paul Offit with the Children's Hospital of Philadelphia. "They care about their health. And they trust their doctors and they believe that they should go to their doctors. And yet they don't go," he said.[24]

The 2013–2015 National Survey of Family Growth found that approximately 7 percent of young people between the ages of fifteen to twenty-five wouldn't seek reproductive health care because they were worried their parents would find out about it. This figure increased in younger participants. Almost 18 percent of teens between the ages of fifteen and seventeen said they wouldn't seek reproductive health care because they didn't want their parents to find out about it. The study also found that when teens visited a doctor but were accompanied by a parent, they were less likely to receive reproductive health services.

Health-care providers are trying to better serve teens. Many professional health organizations also have guidelines on how to talk

During checkups, doctors will often ask teens if they are sexually active. Doctors do this to make sure teens are safe and healthy.

to teens about reproductive health. For example, doctors who belong to these organizations may ask a teen patient's parent to step out of the room so they can speak to the teen privately. Actions such as this are protected by the Health Insurance Portability and Accountability Act (HIPAA), which protects patients' medical information. "That is recognized under the HIPAA privacy rule as having some significance, and affording, then, the young person some protection for those discussions," said Abigail English, director of the Center for Adolescent Health & the Law. "It's important for young people to know that they can consent for certain services on their own and not be afraid to seek services in a confidential way."[25]

Many teenagers are more comfortable talking to their health-care providers about reproductive health if their health-care provider starts the conversation. For that reason, doctors are encouraged to be proactive in talking to teens about the risks of STDs, prevention methods, and STD testing, which is the best tool to reduce the spread of STDs. "By taking a proactive role in their patients' sexual health, health care providers can help reduce disease burden and long-term health consequences of STDs for the youth of today and the future," the website HIV.gov states.[26] HIV.gov is the federal government's primary source for HIV information.

STD Cause and Effect

STDs are caused by sexual activity. They spread further when people do not use appropriate protection, such as consistent and correct condom use, or receive the correct reproductive care. Teens can help themselves by using the necessary protection every time they have sex and by following the medical advice of their health-care providers—including being tested for STDs as health-care providers recommend. STDs are a major public health problem, but they are also a personal health issue that teens can effectively manage.

> "It's important for young people to know that they can consent for certain services on their own and not be afraid to seek services in a confidential way."[25]
>
> —Abigail English, director of the Center for Adolescent Health & the Law

Chapter 3

WHAT ARE THE EFFECTS OF STDS?

Some STDs are only mild annoyances that can be easily cured with treatment. Other STDs, if not properly treated, can cause long-term health problems, permanent damage, and even death. Both types of STDs can also affect people psychologically. The diseases' symptoms or the social stigma associated with STDs may cause people emotional stress. STDs may also impact people's relationships. In addition to these personal effects of STDs, the diseases affect society at large. As a public health issue, STDs and their treatment lead to additional costs for the health-care system.

Pelvic Inflammatory Disease

One of the most common long-term problems associated with untreated STDs is pelvic inflammatory disease (PID), an infection that affects a woman's reproductive organs. Approximately 4 percent of sexually active women between the ages of eighteen and forty-four has had PID. This condition can be caused by infections that are not STDs. However, it is often a complication of chlamydia and gonorrhea, which are the main causes of PID. They make up as many as one-third to one-half of all PID cases. About 10 to 15 percent of women with untreated chlamydia develop symptomatic PID.

Abdominal pain is felt between the pelvis and ribs. This pain can occur if a person has an STD.

PID causes severe abdominal and pelvic pain, vomiting, and fever. Other symptoms may include an unusual discharge or bad odor from the vagina, pain and/or bleeding during sex, a burning sensation with urination, and bleeding between periods. If caught early, PID can be treated with antibiotics. Women with PID should not participate in sexual activity until their treatment is finished. They and their sexual partners should also be tested and treated for any STDs that may have led to their PID infection.

Though PID can be cured with antibiotics, this treatment cannot undo any damage PID may have already done to the woman's reproductive system. The longer women wait to get PID treated, the more likely they will have complications from their PID. The most common PID complications are the development of scar tissue inside and outside the fallopian tubes, long-term pelvic and abdominal pain, and infertility.

Long-Term Effects of Herpes and HPV

Viral infections such as herpes and HPV cannot be cured. The American Sexual Health Association (ASHA), a nonprofit that promotes sexual health, has said that having a chronic condition of this sort can be stressful. "Too often, we see health as an all-or-nothing proposition: someone with a chronic infection is deemed unhealthy and somehow 'imperfect,'" the organization states on its website. "In reality, everyone faces a host of physical challenges as inevitable as life itself. The task is to meet them and get past them."[27]

> **"In reality, everyone faces a host of physical challenges as inevitable as life itself. The task is to meet them and get past them."[27]**
>
> —American Sexual Health Association

Though herpes cannot be cured, people with the infection can take prescribed medication to try to prevent frequent outbreaks. People can also manage the symptoms of herpes outbreaks with at-home measures. "Warm baths may give some pain relief," suggested Cullins. "Keep the sores dry—moisture can slow healing. Holding cool compresses or ice packs to the sores may be soothing. Pain relievers such as aspirin, acetaminophen, or ibuprofen may help relieve discomfort and fever."[28]

As with herpes, there is no cure for HPV, but there are treatments for the conditions it causes, such as genital warts. If left untreated, genital warts may go away on their own, stay the same, or get larger and increase in number. In some cases, people may choose to have their warts removed by a doctor or with genital wart treatments that can be used at home. Most genital warts respond to treatment within three months. However, it is common for genital warts to return after treatment, especially for the first three months after the treatment.

In addition to genital warts, certain strains of sexually-transmitted HPV can cause cancer. There are more than one hundred types of HPV, and at least thirteen of them are known to cause cancer. According to the National Cancer Institute, HPV causes 95 percent of anal cancers; 70 percent of oropharyngeal cancers, which affect the middle part of the throat, the base of the tongue, and the tonsils; 65 percent of vaginal cancers; 50 percent of vulvar cancers; and 35 percent of penile cancers. HPV also causes almost all cases of cervical cancer, which is the most common HPV-related disease. Cervical cancer is also the fourth most frequently occurring cancer in women worldwide. In the United States 4,000 women die each year from cervical cancer.

Long-Term Effects of HIV and Hepatitis B

Like HPV, the viral infections HIV and hepatitis B are known to lead to serious and potentially fatal health problems. There is no cure for HIV, so treatment focuses on controlling the virus's progress and symptoms. HIV progresses in three stages. The first stage is the acute stage of the infection, which has flu-like symptoms. In the second stage, the virus is still developing in the body, but people will likely experience no symptoms. This stage is also referred to as asymptomatic HIV infection or chronic HIV infection. If people with HIV receive proper treatment at this stage, their HIV may not progress to its final stage, AIDS.

However, if HIV is not treated, the disease will continue to attack a person's immune system, especially its T cells. These are white blood cells that help protect people from infection. They are an important part of the immune system, and if they fall below a certain level in a

person's body, the symptoms of AIDS appear. These symptoms include weight loss, fatigue, night sweats, fever, headaches, diarrhea, loss of appetite, and swollen lymph nodes. At this point, people will also develop what are called opportunistic infections. These are infections that happen more often in people with weakened immune systems. They also affect these individuals more severely. Since the AIDS epidemic started in the early 1980s, more than 1.2 million people have been diagnosed with AIDS in the United States. People with AIDS usually survive three years without treatment. But if they get a serious opportunistic illness, their life expectancy is just one year.

Cirrhosis, **bottom,** *is a serious health condition. It occurs when the liver is damaged and scarred.*

Like HIV, hepatitis B can cause life-threatening complications such as liver damage, liver cancer, liver failure, and death. However, these complications are less common than those of HIV. In adults, only about one-half of people with recently acquired hepatitis B will show symptoms. When infected with hepatitis B as adults, less than 5 percent of otherwise healthy people will develop a chronic infection. Of these individuals, 20 to 30 percent of them will develop liver cancer, scarring of the liver, known as cirrhosis, or both.

STDs' Effects on Pregnancy and Infants

In addition to causing long-term health problems, STDs can also have devastating consequences throughout pregnancy and during the infancy of a child. For example, trichomoniasis and gonorrhea are related to premature delivery and low birth weights. Gonorrhea during pregnancy is also linked to an infection of the amniotic fluid and placental tissues; postpartum sepsis, a possibly deadly inflammatory response to infection; and secondary infertility, which is when a woman can't get pregnant or carry a baby to term after she's already had a child. A mother's herpes infection during pregnancy can cause low birth weight in infants, premature delivery, and stillbirth.

Bacterial and parasitic STDs such as gonorrhea, syphilis, chlamydia, and trichomoniasis can be safely treated with antibiotics during pregnancy. Viral STDs such as herpes can't be cured, but they may be managed with antiviral medications during pregnancy to reduce the risk of passing the disease to the infant. Antivirals are medicines that work against viruses, similar to the way antibiotics work against bacteria. They can decrease disease symptoms, but they cannot completely eliminate the infection.

Some STDs can also be passed from mothers to infants during childbirth. When diseases are spread this way, they are called congenital. These types of STD infections can cause serious health problems. For example, infants with congenital gonorrhea may develop joint infections, blood infections, and eye infections which can lead to blindness. Congenital chlamydia can cause pink eye and pneumonia in infants. HPV, when passed on this way, can cause warts to develop on an infant's larynx, eyes, or genitals.

Most newborns who become infected by congenital hepatitis B don't have immediate symptoms. However, they have a 90 percent chance of developing chronic hepatitis B. In recent years, congenital syphilis has become an increasing problem. During 2016, there were more than 620 cases of congenital syphilis reported in the United States. These infections led to serious health complications and, if left untreated, resulted in approximately 40 percent of infant deaths. Since syphilis is a bacterial STD, these deaths could have been prevented. "Every baby born with syphilis represents a tragic public health system failure," said Bolan. "All it takes is a simple STD test and antibiotic treatment to prevent this tragedy from occurring."[29]

> **"Every baby born with syphilis represents a tragic public health system failure. All it takes is a simple STD test and antibiotic treatment to prevent this tragedy from occurring."[29]**
>
> —Dr. Gail Bolan, director of CDC's Division of STD Prevention

The CDC recommends pregnant women be tested and treated for STDs because the earlier pregnant women receive this care the "better the health outcomes will be" for both mother and baby.[30] Since some STDs can be transmitted to a baby during a vaginal childbirth, many women with HIV or other STDs choose to have a cesarean section to reduce this risk. In a cesarean section procedure, surgeons cut into the mother's abdomen to remove the baby, rather than allowing it to pass through the vagina.

Emotional Effect of STD Diagnosis

People with STDs that have long-term symptoms and people with easily-curable STDs are both likely to have emotional reactions to their diagnoses. For many people, emotional distress is associated with their STD diagnosis. According to the Mayo Clinic, this experience in and of itself is "traumatic."[31] Receiving an STD diagnosis may be particularly hard for people with viral STDs that have no cure.

People can be shocked when they learn they have an STD. Many people also worry that they will be judged by their peers.

A herpes diagnosis, for example, has been shown to cause psychological distress. ASHA states on its website that, "Herpes may raise strong emotional issues, especially in the first few weeks or months after a diagnosis."[32] In a 2017 *Teen Vogue* article, one woman shared her reaction to her herpes diagnosis. "The months following the diagnosis were the worst of my life," the woman wrote. "I fell into a deep depression. . . . I felt dirty and lonely. I was convinced I would be alone forever." However, her perspective and her life changed, in part when she realized that she was not alone. She reminded herself that as many as one in six Americans between the ages of fourteen and forty-nine have herpes caused by HSV-2 and still more have herpes caused by HSV-1. The writer reported that she has since adjusted to her diagnosis. "I am now in a happy, committed relationship with

> **"Most people get an STD at least once, and millions are living with STDs now. The reality is that STDs can happen to anybody who's ever been sexual with someone, which is almost everybody on earth."[34]**
>
> —Planned Parenthood

my boyfriend, who knows of my diagnosis and loves me just the same," she wrote. "I take my medication daily and he gets tested regularly. He hasn't contracted the virus, and he doesn't—and never did—think I was 'gross.'"[33]

If people are feeling overwhelmed or distressed after their STD diagnosis, they should reach out for help. People can confide in a romantic partner, close friend, or family member. Likewise, counselors and therapists can offer support and guidance. Many online and in-person support groups for people with STDs are also available. Support groups can give people a safe environment to talk about their STDs with people in similar situations—and there are plenty of these people. Planned Parenthood notes on its website that STDs are far more common than many people realize. "Most people get an STD at least once, and millions are living with STDs now," the organization has said. "The reality is that STDs can happen to anybody who's ever been sexual with someone, which is almost everybody on earth."[34]

STDs and Social Stigma

When people have strong emotional reactions to STD diagnoses, they may be experiencing the effects of social stigma. "Growing up in our society, most of us come to view a sexually transmitted disease as a fate that befalls only those who have done something wrong," ASHA notes on its website.[35] That may lead people with STDs to think that people are judging them for their behavior because they have an STD.

Society holds girls to different standards than boys. Girls can face harsh stigma from peers when it comes to their sexual activity.

"Unfortunately, STDs carry enormous stigma in this country, and it's hard for people to come forward for treatment," said David Harvey, executive director of the National Coalition of STD Directors, which is a public health group.[36] This relationship between STD-related stigma and people's readiness to seek testing for STDs was the subject of a study published in the journal *Perspectives on Sexual and Reproductive Health* in 2009. For this study, researchers interviewed more than 500 people between the ages of fifteen and twenty-four about their perception of STD-related stigma and whether they had been tested for STDs in the past year. The study found that both male and female participants were less likely to have been tested for an STD if they had higher perceptions of STD-related stigma.

Worries about social stigma may also affect teens when they do decide to speak to their health-care providers. Teens may worry that their health-care providers will judge them for being irresponsible or immoral, so they may not be honest with them about their sexual health or history. For this reason, health-care providers like Dr. Alyssa Dweck, a gynecologist, try to focus on educating patients about STDs, while reminding them that these infections are very common. "While normalizing STIs is tough, reassuring patients that they are not alone is very helpful in an effort to destigmatize," she said.[37]

HOW TO NOTIFY SEXUAL PARTNERS ABOUT STDS

Teens with STDs must tell their past and current sexual partners about their STD diagnoses. This is an important step to prevent the spread of STDs. Though this conversation may seem awkward, there are steps people can take to make it easier on themselves and their partners.

For starters, people should come into the conversation prepared. Before telling their sexual partners about STD diagnoses, people should make sure they have all the facts. Their partners need to know the exact diagnosis so they can take the steps needed to protect themselves. When notifying someone about an STD diagnosis, people should also try to be as straightforward and honest as possible. Ideally, the conversation should also take place in an environment where both people feel comfortable and won't be interrupted.

Notifying past sexual partners may prove more difficult, especially if people no longer have a positive relationship with them. If people are concerned about their safety when notifying sexual partners about an STD, they should consider contacting them through email, text, or phone call, rather than an in-person conversation. In serious instances where people think they may be in danger from a sexual partner, they should contact national domestic violence hotlines for help.

STDs and Relationships

When people are diagnosed with STDs, they may worry that it will prevent them from having romantic relationships. Some people who are in a relationship with the person who gave them the STD may also be reluctant to leave that relationship. They might be worried about telling future partners about their STD status and being rejected.

Dr. Michael Krychman, the executive director at the Southern California Center for Sexual Health and Survivorship, said many people with STDs "become increasingly concerned about relationships and trust after they have had an STI. . . . As an extreme, some patients avoid sex all together."[38] It doesn't have to be this way. Jenelle Marie Davis is the founder of the STD Project, an organization created to reduce the stigma attached to STDs. She said many people call the STD Project after they receive a STD diagnosis because they're worried about how it will affect their relationships. "Folks just believe that they will never be able to date again," Davis said. "It's terrifying initially."[39]

Though some people with STDs may worry about dating, they don't need to. STDs don't usually prevent people from having successful, long-term romantic relationships. This is especially true if people are honest with their partners about their STDs. Experts agree that telling current and former sexual partners about STD infections is important. Not only does notifying sexual partners help reduce the spread of STDs by allowing all partners to receive necessary treatment, but it can also build trust in relationships.

Dr. Edward W. Hook with the University of Alabama at Birmingham Medical Center said these conversations may be hard to have, but they are a "great basis for starting a relationship." He said people shouldn't be embarrassed about talking to romantic partners about their STDs, because they are just a health problem like the flu.

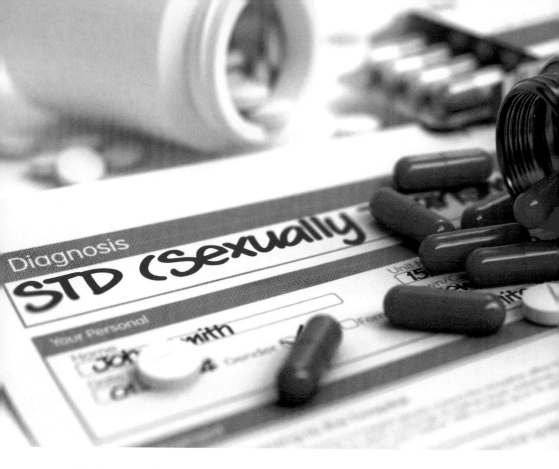

People can receive medication after they get an STD. Medicine will help people treat their illness.

"We take vitamins for our health, we go to the doctor's office for checkups, and nobody has any trouble talking about that," he said.[40]

The Economic Cost of STDs

STDs not only affect the person with the infection and those in relationships with them, they also affect society as a whole. STDs and their treatment put a strain on health-care industries. In the United States, there are roughly 20 million new STD infections each year. These infections come with a cost. In February 2013, the CDC published a study looking into what it called the "severe human and economic burden" STDs have on the United States.[41] Its study looked at eight common STDs: chlamydia, gonorrhea, hepatitis B, herpes

(HSV-2), HPV, HIV, syphilis, and trichomoniasis. It estimated that the lifetime cost of treating these STDs contracted in a single year is $15.6 billion.

Viral STDs, such as HIV, cost the health-care system the most. Since they cannot be cured, they have to be treated throughout someone's life, leading to more treatment costs. Likewise, HPV is also expensive because it can lead to cancers which are costly to treat. However, the cost of curable STDs is high as well because they are so common. Chlamydia is the most common curable STD. Even though it is relatively inexpensive to treat an individual with this disease, the sheer number of patients means it is the most expensive STD for the health-care system to treat.

When compiling its report, the CDC only looked at direct medical costs per case of the eight common STDs. It did not include indirect costs, such as loss of productivity, or costs that cannot be calculated, such as emotional pain and suffering.

These Costs Can Be Prevented

There are multiple STD prevention tools available for teens. By using protection such as condoms during all sexual acts and by getting reproductive health care when needed, teens can avoid catching STDs. If teens have an STD, they can help prevent its spread by notifying all current and past sexual partners about their diagnosis. All of these individual steps can help reduce the effects of these worldwide health problems.

Chapter 4

HOW ARE STDS PREVENTED AND TREATED?

The only 100 percent proven way to avoid getting STDs is to practice abstinence. According to Planned Parenthood, "Abstinence is a great way to avoid the risks that come with sex—like pregnancy and STDs—until you're ready to prevent and/or handle them."[42] But if teens do decide to become sexually active, there are several ways they can reduce their STD risk. The CDC has said that teens "have more power than anyone to prevent teen pregnancy and sexually transmitted diseases."[43] In order to protect themselves and others from STDs, teens need to use safer sex practices. Experts prefer the term *safer sex* instead of *safe sex* because sexual intercourse is never completely risk free.

Safer Sex and Relationships

In its YRBS report released in 2015, the CDC found that almost 12 percent of high school students had sexual intercourse with more than four people. In general, the fewer sexual partners someone has, the less risk they have of catching an STD. However, no matter how many sexual partners someone has, it is always a good idea for partners to get STD tests at the start of new relationships. But that is just one step people should take to practice safer sex.

People should have open and honest communication with their partners before having sex. This can help them avoid STDs.

Before engaging in sexual activity, people should also talk to their sexual partner about whether they should wait to have sex, how sex might affect their relationship, and about the shared responsibility of preventing pregnancy and STDs. Jeralyn Perkins, a health educator with Weber-Morgan Health Department in Odgen, Utah, said these are the sort of topics health-care professionals should address with teens. "As educators, there's a lot we can do to empower youth to have successful futures. . . . Are we really helping them think critically about all the consequences [of sex]?" she asked. "Are they prepared to handle how being sexually active affects all their relationships? What if they're expecting commitment and their partner doesn't reciprocate?"[44]

Teens can address these issues with their partners by talking about them and by sharing their sexual history. Before engaging in any type of sexual activity, partners should discuss whether they or any of their past partners has ever had an STD, when they had the STD, and if it ever came back. They should also discuss how many sexual partners each of them has had and what they have done or not done to practice safer sex in those relationships.

STD Testing and Exams

Like many people, teens may believe the misconception that they would always be able to tell who has an STD simply by looking at them. That's not the case. "You can't tell if someone has an STD by their looks," explained Dr. Abdur-Rahman. He also noted that same principle applies to people's genitals. "I've had patients tell me before having sex with someone, they do a quick examination to make sure everything looks 'normal,'" Dr. Abdur-Rahman said. "Outside of an active outbreak of herpes or genital warts, the majority of the time you won't see any visual evidence [of an STD]. But if someone has it, they can still transmit it."[45]

> **"Outside of an active outbreak of herpes or genital warts, the majority of the time you won't see any visual evidence [of an STD]. But if someone has it, they can still transmit it."[45]**
>
> —Dr. Idries Abdur-Rahman, ob-gyn

Since so many STDs don't present symptoms that people can see or feel, they frequently aren't discovered until people test for them. Traysa Smith, a certified physician's assistant, said this is something she sees often in her teen patients. "More common than not, my patients are asymptomatic, and we find an STI as part of their routine screening," she said. "It's part of their routine annual exam."[46] In addition to getting checked for STDs during annual exams, sexually active teens should also get tested for STDs if they notice common STD symptoms such as vaginal or urethral discharge or genital irritation.

When people realize they need an STD test, there are several places they can go to for help. People can get STD tests at their regular health-care provider's office, community health clinics, and Planned Parenthood health centers. The cost of STD testing varies depending on where people go, what sort of tests they need, and whether or not they have health insurance. Some government programs and clinics also provide free or inexpensive STD tests based on people's income levels.

CONFIDENTIAL STD TESTING

Many teens worry about getting reproductive health care, including STD tests, because they are afraid their parents may find out. However, there are laws in place that protect teens' privacy when they discuss things with their doctors. In every state and the District of Columbia, teens can get confidential STD testing and medical care. When teens receive confidential services, their health information cannot be shared with anyone without their permission. Most US states allow teens to receive HIV tests and counseling without parental consent, and some states allow teens to consent to vaccinations. Many states also allow minors to receive confidential contraception services, as well.

Confidentiality laws go a long way to protect teen patients' privacy. However, there are still some ways that parents may find out about a teen's reproductive health care. For example, if STD testing or treatment is billed to an insurance company, the policy owner may find out. If the policy owner is the teen's parent, the teen's treatment may show up on the parent's insurance paperwork.

Each STD has its own test, and based on people's symptoms, doctors will prescribe the tests that are right for them. Also, because some STDs look alike, a doctor may recommend people get tested for multiple infections. STD tests are performed in different ways since STDs can be detected in people's urine, blood, saliva, or in samples of their cells. For urine-based STD tests, patients urinate in a cup while at the doctor's office. For blood-based STD tests, a nurse or doctor usually takes blood from a patient's arm or uses a simple finger prick to get a blood sample. HIV tests are done by rubbing a soft cotton swab on the inside of a patient's cheek to collect saliva. If a patient has sores or blisters, a doctor may also take a sample of fluid from them using a cotton swab. In some cases, a doctor may be able to tell if a patient has an STD just by doing a physical examination. This is especially true in cases where there are obvious warts, sores, irritation, rashes, or discharge.

Some STD tests show results in as little as twenty minutes, while other STD tests may take a few days or weeks to show results. That is because these tests often need to be sent off to a lab for analysis. If a patient does not hear back from a doctor about their STD test, they shouldn't simply assume everything is fine. Instead, they should call their doctor and confirm their test results.

When people with STD symptoms visit a health-care provider, the provider will often do more than simply administer an STD test. The provider may also ask questions about the patient's sexual history. Collecting this information can help better inform the health-care provider about the patient's risk factors so the provider can prescribe more targeted tests and treatment. For example, the provider might ask the patient about when the sexual activity happened, the gender of the patient's sexual partner, their relationship with the sexual partner, and the sexual partner's symptoms or previous STDs. Additionally, the physician may ask specific questions about the sexual activity itself, including whether or not protection was used and what type of sexual contact it was, such as oral, vaginal, or anal.

Since the nature of these questions is very personal, patients may be much more comfortable discussing these things with a health-care provider they trust. Though these conversations may seem awkward, Planned Parenthood urges patients not to be embarrassed. They want people to remember that "doctors have seen and heard it all. Most people get an STD at least once in their lives, and getting tested is the responsible thing to do—it means you're taking good care of your health."[47]

"Doctors have seen and heard it all. Most people get an STD at least once in their lives, and getting tested is the responsible thing to do—it means you're taking good care of your health."[47]

—Planned Parenthood

Treatment for Chlamydia

If a person's STD test comes back positive, he or she will be given treatment based on their specific STD diagnosis. Treatments vary based on whether the infection is bacterial, viral, or parasitic, and on how advanced the infection is. Many bacterial and parasitic infections can be easily cured with medication.

Chlamydia is one STD that can be treated with antibiotics. However, the treatment of this common infection can be complicated by several factors. For example, chlamydia infections are hard to treat because they are hard to identify. Since many chlamydia infections are asymptomatic, people may have chlamydia for months or years without realizing it. The infection will remain in people's bodies until it is treated with antibiotics.

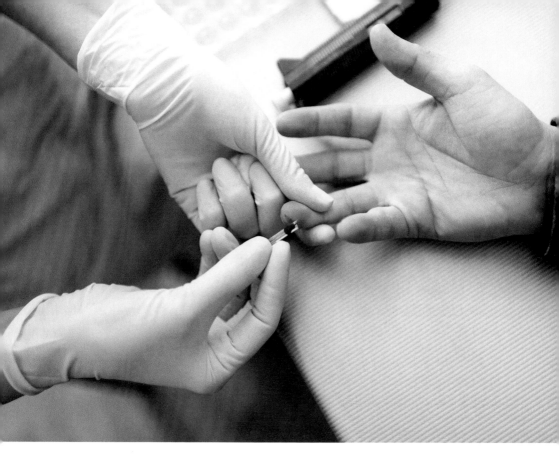

Blood tests can show whether a person has chlamydia. If they do, doctors can recommend treatment options.

Another factor that complicates the treatment of chlamydia is its resemblance and connection to gonorrhea. Chlamydia is often confused with gonorrhea, and vice versa, so doctors often recommend people get tested for both. Many people also end up having both infections at the same time so they are prescribed antibiotics for both diseases, which can be taken simultaneously.

Treatment for Gonorrhea

Though gonorrhea can typically be cured with medication, in recent years the bacteria that causes it has been evolving to become antibiotic resistant. Diseases that are antibiotic resistant are not affected by the drugs used to treat them. The disease is not killed by the medicine, and instead, it continues to reproduce. Antibiotic resistance is something health professionals have to worry about with all antibiotics. That's because the more often bacteria are exposed to a certain type of antibiotic, the quicker the bacteria evolves its defenses to that antibiotic, decreasing the medicine's effectiveness.

"The bacteria that cause gonorrhea are particularly smart," explained Teodora Wi, WHO medical officer. "Every time we use a new class of antibiotics to treat the infection, the bacteria evolve to resist them."[48] According to the CDC, "Thirty percent of new gonorrhea infections each year are resistant to at least one drug."[49] In the majority of countries, there is now only one type of antibiotics, cephalosporins, that are able to successfully treat gonorrhea infections.

The CDC has named antibiotic resistant gonorrhea an urgent health threat and has been encouraging the development of new drugs to treat the disease. To ensure that these drugs don't also become ineffective, the Global Antibiotic Research and Development Partnership has set aside $50 million for research and development in gonorrhea treatment. Zoliflodacin, a new type of antibiotic, developed by the company Entasis, has shown promise in treating gonorrhea. In 2016, it was found safe and effective in preliminary clinical trials.

Treatment for Syphilis, Trichomoniasis, and Pubic Lice

As a bacterial infection, syphilis can also be cured by antibiotics, and penicillin is its most common antibiotic treatment. How easily the disease is treated depends on how advanced the infection is. Syphilis is cured more easily in its early stages. If a person has had syphilis for less than one year, they can usually be cured with a single shot of antibiotics. People who have had the infection for longer than a year will require more doses.

Like the other bacterial and parasitic STDs, trichomoniasis and pubic lice can also be easily cured. Trichomoniasis can be treated with antibiotics, and the prescription for trichomoniasis is usually the drug metronidazole. Pubic lice are similarly cured with medicated creams or shampoos.

Treatment for Herpes and HIV

Viral STDs can be treated with antivirals and similar medications, but they cannot be cured. For example, people with herpes can take antiviral medications when they have an outbreak. If these medications are taken as soon as the individual is aware of symptoms, they can reduce the intensity and duration of the outbreak. However, these medications are more effective on the initial herpes outbreak and are less effective during recurrent ones.

Some people with herpes take a low dose of antiviral medication each day rather than at the onset of symptoms. This is called suppressive therapy. In addition to reducing outbreaks, it can also reduce the likelihood that people will transmit herpes to others. This type of therapy may also help with the psychological stress of herpes outbreaks.

Individuals with HIV or who are at a high risk of HIV have a few treatment and prevention options. People who are at high risk of catching HIV can take a pre-exposure prophylaxis drugs (PrEP) pill each day. These pills contain two medicines called tenofovir and emtricitabine, which, when combined with other medicines, can help treat HIV. When people who take PrEP are exposed to HIV, these medicines help prevent the virus from becoming a permanent infection. If people take PrEP consistently, it can reduce their risk of HIV infection by up to 92 percent.

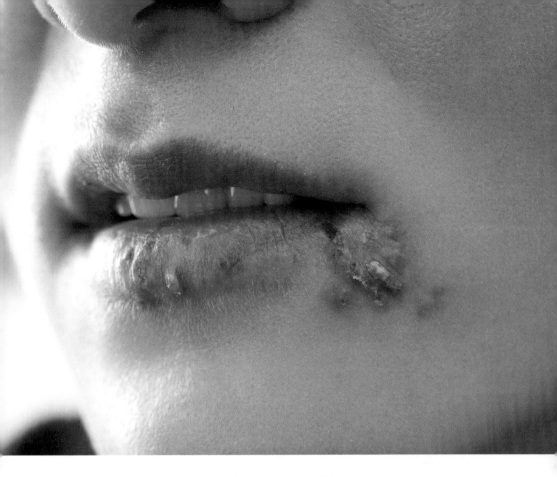

Oral herpes can be very visible during an outbreak. This can cause embarrassment for people who have it.

Antiretroviral therapy (ART) medicines are for people living with HIV. They are called antiretrovirals because HIV is a kind of virus called retrovirus. These drugs are designed to slow the progress of HIV in people's bodies by decreasing the amount of virus in their systems. ART drugs have been available since the 1990s. According to the CDC, they "are the reason why the annual number of deaths related to AIDS has dropped over the past two decades."[50] If taken consistently and correctly, ART keeps people healthy for years and reduces people's likelihood of spreading the virus. People with HIV who use ART therapy may never progress to AIDS. According to HIV.gov, this is because "treatment helps keep the virus in check."[51]

Another treatment and prevention option for HIV is post-exposure prophylaxis (PEP). In PEP, people take ART after they have been exposed to HIV to avoid becoming infected. People have to take PEP within seventy-two hours after they have been potentially exposed to HIV. The sooner the people take PEP after possible infection, the better. People who have been prescribed PEP need to take ART once or twice a day for twenty-eight days. The CDC has stated that when used correctly, PEP is effective in preventing HIV, but it doesn't offer 100 percent protection. ART and PEP can also reduce people's risk of transmitting HIV.

Treatment for Hepatitis B and HPV

Unlike many STDs, hepatitis B and HPV can be prevented using vaccines. Hepatitis B vaccines are usually given as three or four injections over the course of six months. People who know they have been exposed to hepatitis B but aren't sure if they have been vaccinated should contact their health-care provider immediately. Within twelve hours of exposure to the virus, people can be given an antibody. An antibody is a protein produced by the immune system to protect the body from foreign substances called antigens. The body sees many things as antigens such as disease-causing organisms and toxins such as insect venom. Antibodies remove these materials from the body after latching on to them. This is a short-term protection measure, and people will also be given the hepatitis B vaccination as an added precaution.

From there, the treatment of hepatitis B varies depending on what sort of infection it is. Hepatitis B can cause acute and chronic infections. When the infection is acute, it may not require treatment, as it could go away on its own. If an individual has this type of hepatitis B infection, their doctor may just recommend rest and plenty of fluids. In other acute cases, the virus may be more severe and may need

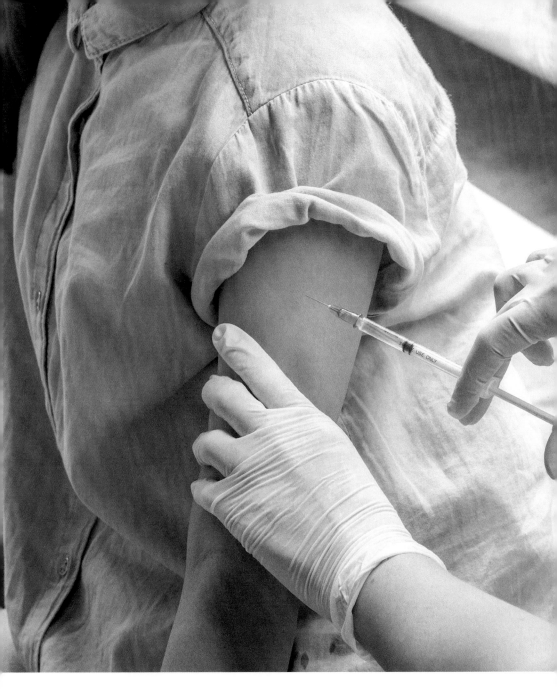

The CDC recommends that children as young as eleven should get the HPV vaccine. This can help their health later on.

to be treated with antiviral drugs during a hospital stay. On the other hand, people with chronic hepatitis B infections need treatment for the rest of their lives. This treatment focuses on reducing the risk of liver disease caused by inflammation of the liver. Treatment also focuses on preventing transmission of the disease to others. The treatment for chronic hepatitis B may include antiviral medications which work against the virus and help protect against damage to the liver. In severe cases of hepatitis B where the liver has been seriously damaged, a patient may require a liver transplant.

As with hepatitis B, there are vaccines to help prevent HPV. The vaccines Cervarix and Gardasil protect people against the types of HPV that cause the majority of cervical cancers. Gardasil also protects people against the HPV strains that cause most genital warts. Since HPV can be spread by intimate skin-to-skin contact, the course of three vaccines needs to be completed before people engage in any kind of sexual activity. For that reason, these vaccines are recommended for boys and girls between the ages of eleven and twelve.

The HPV vaccines work by making antibodies that attach to the virus and stop it from infecting other cells. In the trials that led to their approval, Gardasil and Cervarix were found to provide almost 100 percent protection against cervical infections caused by certain HPV types. However, despite this, these vaccines are not as widely used as people may expect. Among vaccines available for children, HPV vaccines are the most underutilized. There are several reasons for this. One of them is that the vaccine costs about $300 a dose, so in order to do the required three-dose series, people need to pay roughly $1,000. However, most health insurance companies do cover this cost for people since this vaccine is recommended. Another reason for the low usage rate of the HPV vaccine is that some parents believe vaccinating children for HPV at an early age will make them engage in sexual activity earlier. Dr. Debbie Saslow, the director of cancer control intervention for the American Cancer Society disagrees with this theory. "Multiple studies have shown no negative impact on any measure of sexual activity among girls given the HPV vaccine," she said. "You don't tell teenagers learning to drive not to wear a seatbelt because it may encourage them to run red lights."[52]

Though HPV vaccines can prevent people from catching HPV, they cannot treat established HPV infections or any of the diseases caused by HPV. Despite that, these vaccines could still have a huge impact on people's health. According to the National Cancer Institute, "Widespread vaccination with Cervarix or Gardasil has the potential to reduce cervical cancer incidence around the world by as much as two-thirds."[53] But in order for that potential to be reached, as many people as possible must get vaccinated. That's because vaccination doesn't just protect vaccinated people from HPV infection. If a significant percentage of a population gets vaccinated, that also reduces the amount of HPV viruses as a whole. This provides protection for people who haven't been vaccinated. Since there are fewer HPV viruses in circulation, they are also less likely to be infected. This is called herd immunity.

Whatever course of medication an STD requires, whether it is vaccinations or antibiotics, it is important for teens to follow their physician's instructions. It is also important for them to notify their sexual partners about their diagnosis, since they might need treatment too. These simple steps can reduce the spread of STDs and help people feel healthier faster.

> **"Multiple studies have shown no negative impact on any measure of sexual activity among girls given the HPV vaccine."[52]**
>
> —Dr. Debbie Saslow, the director of cancer control intervention for the American Cancer Society

There are many treatment options for STDs. People who get STDs can still have happy, healthy lives.

Teens Protecting Themselves

Planned Parenthood suggests teens think of STDs the same way they would think of any other infection. "If you do get a STD, it doesn't mean you're 'dirty' or a bad person," the organization says on its website. "You're just one of the millions of people who got an infection. And like other infections, there are medicines to help you stay healthy if you do get an STD."[54]

If Olivia could think about her chlamydia this way, it might help her take better care of her health. For example, if she saw chlamydia as just another illness, she may be comfortable talking to her mom about it. From there, either one of them could make Olivia an appointment with her usual health-care provider. During her appointment, Olivia would be given an exam, tested for STDs, and prescribed a treatment for her diagnosis of chlamydia. Since the treatment for chlamydia is a round of antibiotics, Olivia's infection would be cleared quickly. In the meantime, Olivia would avoid sexual activity with her boyfriend, Mason, and she'd inform him of her diagnosis. That would allow him to get treatment too. Together, the two of them could make better choices in the future, reducing their risk of STDs and keeping them both healthy.

> **"If you do get a STD, it doesn't mean you're 'dirty' or a bad person."[54]**
>
> —Planned Parenthood

RECOGNIZING SIGNS OF TROUBLE

How STDs Are Spread

- Vaginal sex
- Anal sex
- Oral sex
- Skin to skin genital contact
- Some STDs, such as pubic lice, can also be spread by contaminated clothing and bedding.

Main STD Symptoms

- Many STDs have no noticeable symptoms.
- The three most common symptoms of STDs are vaginal or urethral discharge and genital lesions.
- Other common STD symptoms are growths, bumps, rashes, or sores on the genitals or anal areas; sharp pain in the lower abdomen; bleeding between menstrual cycles; and pain or burning during urination or sex.
- Some untreated STDs can cause long-term problems such as infertility, chronic pain, cancer, or even death.

How to Prevent STDs

- Practice abstinence.
- Be in a long-term, monogamous relationship with a partner who has been tested and found not to have STDs.
- Talk to sexual partners about their sexual history, including whether they or any of their partners have ever had an STD.
- Use latex condoms during all sexual activity.
- Get vaccinated against HPV and hepatitis B.

ORGANIZATIONS TO CONTACT

American Sexual Health Association

www.ashasexualhealth.org

The American Sexual Health Association is a nonprofit organization that offers information on sexual health.

Centers for Disease Control and Prevention

www.cdc.gov

The Centers for Disease Control and Prevention is a health protection organization that's part of the US Department of Health & Human Services.

HIV.gov

www.hiv.gov

HIV.gov offers information about HIV and services for people with HIV.

Office of Disease Prevention and Health Promotion

www.healthypeople.gov

The Office of Disease Prevention and Health Promotion aims to improve people's health through a number of initiatives.

US Department of Health & Human Services

www.hhs.gov

The US Department of Health & Human Services aims to protect the health of people in the United States by offering health services.

SOURCE NOTES

Introduction: Olivia's Story

1. Quoted in "Adolescents and Young Adults," *CDC*, December 8, 2017. cdc.gov.

2. Quoted in Zahra Barnes, "The 9 Biggest Lies About STDs You Should Stop Believing Now," *Self*, April 21, 2017. self.com.

3. Quoted in "Abstinence and Outercourse," *Planned Parenthood*, n.d. plannedparenthood.org.

4. Quoted in Vera Papisova, "The 5 Most Common STDs Among Teens," *TeenVogue*, July 21, 2015. teenvogue.com.

5. Quoted in Alexandra Sifferlin, "Here's Why Teen STDs Are Hitting All-Time Highs," *Time*, November 7, 2016. time.com.

Chapter 1: What Are STDs?

6. Quoted in Julie H. Case, "Everything You Need to Know About Chlamydia Symptoms in Women," *Woman's Day*, September 6, 2017. womansday.com.

7. Quoted in Kenneth L Stewart and Casey Jones, "Pathways to Progress: Women's Health Services in West Texas Gauged," *GoSanAngelo*, February 9, 2018. gosanangelo.com.

8. Quoted in Sandee LaMotte, "New STD Cases Hit Record High in US, CDC Says," *CNN*, September 28, 2017. cnn.com.

9. Quoted in LaMotte, "New STD Cases Hit Record High in US, CDC Says."

10. Quoted in Vera Papisova, "The 5 Most Common STDs Among Teens," *TeenVogue*, July 21, 2015. teenvogue.com.

11. Quoted in Angela Haupt, "6 Herpes Symptoms in Women That Shouldn't Be Ignored," *Women's Health*, n.d. womenshealthmag.com.

12. Quoted in "Living with Herpes: 10 Things to Know, from Someone Who Has It," *TeenVogue*, November 21, 2017. teenvogue.com.

13. Quoted in "Living with Herpes: 10 Things to Know, from Someone Who Has It."

14. Quoted in "Bacterial Vaginosis—CDC Fact Sheet," *CDC*, February 16, 2017. cdc.gov.

15. Quoted in Zahra Barnes, "Seriously, What's the Best Way to Clean My Vagina?" *Self*, March 3, 2018. self.com.

Chapter 2: What Causes STDs?

16. Quoted in Zahra Barnes, "The 9 Biggest Lies About STDs You Should Stop Believing Now," *Self*, April 21, 2017. self.com.

17. Quoted in Ronnie Cohen, "Kids Aren't Protecting Themselves Against STDs During Oral Sex," *Reuters*, December 6, 2017. reuters.com.

18. Quoted in Arti Patel, "Canadian Teens Need to Be More Aware of STIs—And It Starts with Sex Ed," *Global News*, October 22, 2017. globalnews.ca.

19. Quoted in John Enger, "Report: Teen Pregnancies Are Down, But Gonorrhea Is Up," *MPR News*, June 14, 2017. mprnews.org.

20. Quoted in "Condom Effectiveness," *CDC*, n.d. cdc.gov.

21. Quoted in Ronnie Cohen, "Kids Aren't Protecting Themselves Against STDs During Oral Sex."

22. Quoted in "HIV/AIDS," *CDC*, October 27, 2016. cdc.gov.

23. Quoted in Meredith Newman, "4 Things to Know About Getting Teens Tested As STI Rates Rise in Delaware," *Delaware Online*, August 22, 2017. delawareonline.com.

24. Quoted in Maggie Fox, "Meningitis Vaccine Protects Against Gonorrhea, Too," *NBC News*, July 11, 2017. nbcnews.com.

25. Quoted in Karen Pallarito, "Why Some Teens Won't Talk to Their Doctor About Sexual Health Issues," *CBC News*, December 19, 2016. cbsnews.com.

26. Quoted in "Encouraging Health Care Providers to Reach Youth for STD Awareness Month," *HIV.gov*, April 17, 2012. hiv.gov.

Chapter 3: What Are the Effects of STDs?

27. Quoted in "Emotional Issues," *American Sexual Health Association*, n.d. ashasexualhealth.org.

28. Quoted in Vera Papisova, "The 5 Most Common STDs Among Teens," *TeenVogue*, July 21, 2015. teenvogue.com.

29. Quoted in Sandee LaMotte, "New STD Cases Hit Record High in US, CDC Says," *CNN*, September 28, 2017. cnn.com.

30. Quoted in "STDs during Pregnancy—CDC Fact Sheet," *CDC*, n.d. cdc.gov.

31. Quoted in "Sexually Transmitted Diseases (STDs)," *Mayo Clinic*, n.d. mayoclinic.org.

32. Quoted in "Emotional Issues."

33. Quoted in "Living with Herpes: 10 Things to Know, from Someone Who Has It," *TeenVogue*, November 21, 2017. teenvogue.com.

34. Quoted in "Get Tested," *Planned Parenthood*, n.d. plannedparenthood.org.

35. Quoted in "Emotional Issues."

36. Quoted in LaMotte, "New STD Cases Hit Record High in US, CDC Says."

37. Quoted in Kyli Rodriguez-Cayro, "Is Gonorrhea Antibiotic Resistant? Some Strains Are, But Here's Why Panicking About It Does More Harm Than Good," *Bustle*, December 1, 2017. bustle.com.

38. Quoted in Rodriguez-Cayro, "Is Gonorrhea Antibiotic Resistant? Some Strains Are, But Here's Why Panicking About It Does More Harm Than Good."

39. Quoted in Alison Bowen, "Dating with an STI: How to Manage the Conversation," *Chicago Tribune*, September 15, 2015. chicagotribune.com.

40. Quoted in Bowen, "Dating with an STI: How to Manage the Conversation."

41. Quoted in "Incidence, Prevalence, and Cost of Sexually Transmitted Infections in the United States," *CDC*, February 2013. cdc.gov.

Chapter 4: How Are STDs Prevented and Treated?

42. Quoted in "Abstinence and Outercourse," *Planned Parenthood*, n.d. plannedparenthood.org.

43. Quoted in "Reproductive Health: Teen Pregnancy," *CDC*, March 3, 2016. cdc.gov.

44. Quoted in Cathy McKitrick, "Chlamydia, Gonorrhea on the Rise Nationwide and Here in Northern Utah," *Standard-Examiner*, November 14, 2017. standard.net.

45. Quoted in Zahra Barnes, "The 9 Biggest Lies About STDs You Should Stop Believing Now," *Self*, April 21, 2017. self.com.

46. Quoted in McKitrick, "Chlamydia, Gonorrhea on the Rise Nationwide and Here in Northern Utah."

47. Quoted in "Get Tested," *Planned Parenthood*, n.d. plannedparenthood.org.

48. Quoted in Rachel Feltman, "Antibiotic-Resistant Gonorrhea Is a Huge Problem, and It's Only Getting Worse," *Popular Science*, July 10, 2017. popsci.com.

49. Quoted in "Combating the Threat of Antibiotic-Resistant Gonorrhea," *CDC*, February 15, 2018. cdc.gov.

50. Quoted in "HIV Treatment," *CDC*, February 8, 2016. cdc.gov.

51. Quoted in "What Are HIV and AIDS?" *HIV.gov*, May 15, 2017. hiv.gov.

52. Quoted in Jane E Brody, "The Underused HPV Vaccine," *New York Times*, August 22, 2016. well.blogs.nytimes.com.

53. Quoted in "Human Papillomavirus (HPV) Vaccines," *National Cancer Institute*, November 2, 2016. cancer.gov.

54. Quoted in "What Do I Need to Know About STDs?" *Planned Parenthood*, n.d. plannedparenthood.org.

FOR FURTHER RESEARCH

BOOKS

Jill Grimes, *Seductive Delusions: How Everyday People Catch STIs*. Baltimore, MD: Johns Hopkins UP, 2016.

Nat Cotts, *How Do AIDS & Science Connect?* Vestal, NY: Village Earth Press, 2014.

Roman Espejo, ed., *AIDS*. Detroit, MI: Greenhaven, 2012.

Roman Espejo, ed., *Sexually Transmitted Diseases*. Detroit, MI: Greenhaven, 2011.

Terri Dougherty, *Sexually Transmitted Diseases*. Farmington Hills, MI: Lucent Books, 2010.

INTERNET SOURCES

CDC, *STDs in Adolescents and Young Adults*, September 26, 2017. www.cdc.gov.

Sandee LaMotte, "New STD Cases Hit Record High in US, CDC Says," *CNN*, September 28, 2017. www.cnn.com.

MedlinePlus, *Sexually Transmitted Diseases*, n.d. medlineplus.gov.

Karen Pallarito, "Why Some Teens Won't Talk to Their Doctor about Sexual Health Issues," *CBS News*, December 19, 2016. www.cbsnews.com.

WEBSITES

Go Ask Alice!

www.goaskalice.columbia.edu

The site allows people to submit questions on the following: alcohol and drugs, emotional health, nutrition, physical activity, general health, relationships, and sexual and reproductive health.

I Wanna Know

www.iwannaknow.org

I Wanna Know is run by the nonprofit American Sexual Health Association. This website provides sexual health information for teens and young adults.

Planned Parenthood

www.plannedparenthood.org

This is the main website of Planned Parenthood, which provides affordable health care and sex education. It offers information about sex and relationships, pregnancy, and sexually transmitted diseases.

INDEX

IMAGE CREDITS

ABOUT THE AUTHOR

Ashley Strehle Hartman is a journalist and writer. She has written for state health departments and community hospitals. When she's not writing for work, she's writing for fun. She writes an entertainment column for a local newspaper and blogs about baking. She lives in Nebraska with her husband and their dog.